Count!

Denise Fleming

SCHOLASTIC INC.

New York   Toronto   London   Auckland   Sydney

Hello, gnu!

one
gnu

**two
zebras**

Jump, zebras!

3

three
crocodiles

No,

no,

crocodiles!

**four
kangaroos**

Bounce, kangaroos!

five
giraffes

Stretch, giraffes!

6

six
cranes

Quiet, cranes!

seven
worms

Wiggle, worms!

8

eight
toucans

Share, toucans!

nine
fish

Swim, fish!

**ten
lizards**

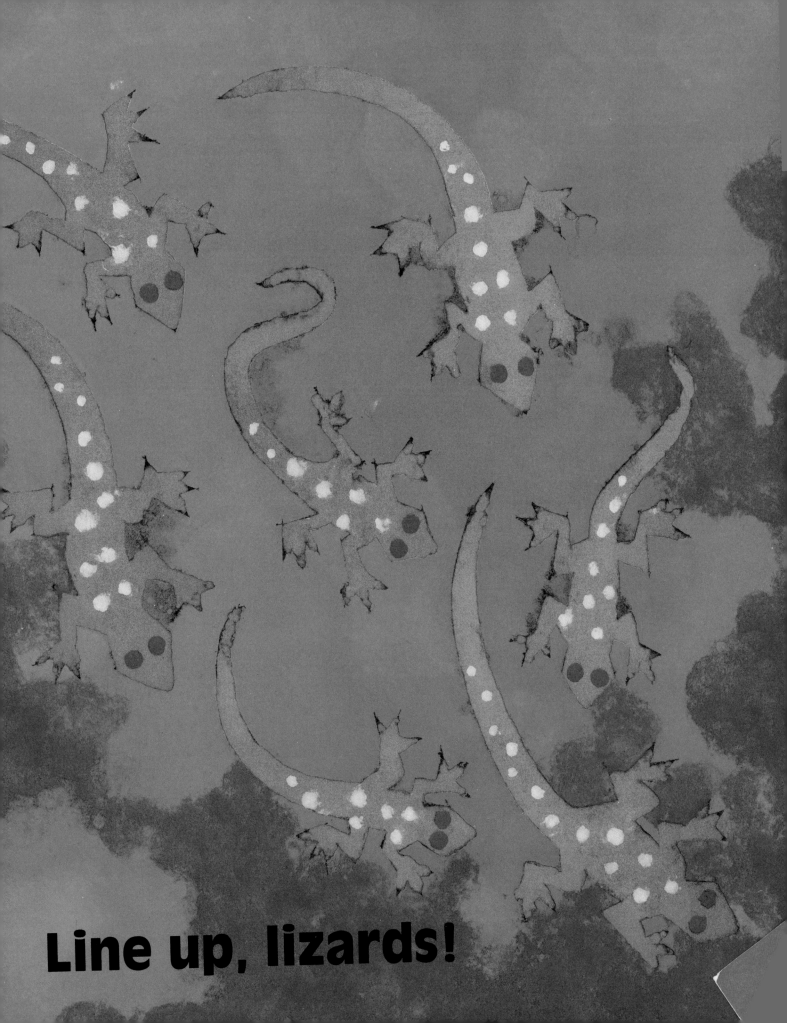

Line up, lizards!

Count again!

Now by tens...

10

ten
lizards

20

twenty
butterflies

**Flutter,
butterflies!**

30

thirty
snails

Slow down, snails!

40

forty
frogs

Leap, frogs!

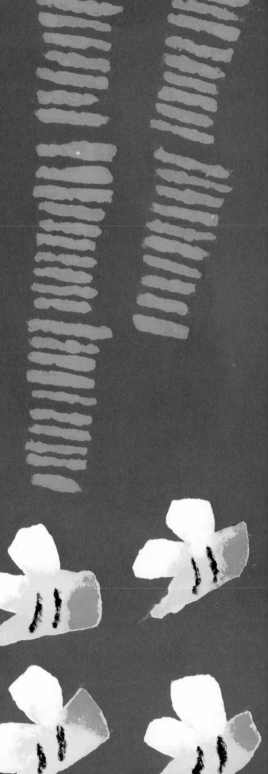

fifty
bees

Bye, bye, bees!

Count again, please!

1 2 3 4 5

6 7 8 9 10

10 20 30

40 50

For my daughter, Indigo
_x x o o_

Copyright © 1992 by Denise Fleming.
All rights reserved. Published by Scholastic Inc.
730 Broadway, New York, NY 10003, by arrangement with Henry Holt and Company, Inc.

12 11 10 9 8 7 6 5 4 3 2 1   3 4 5 6 7 8/9

Printed in the U.S.A.   08

First Scholastic printing, January 1993